D0454225

UNDERSTANDING 99% OF ARTIFICIAL NEURAL NETWORKS
Introduction & Tricks

Marcelo Bosque

Writers Club Press
San Jose New York Lincoln Shanghai

UNDERSTANDING 99% OF ARTIFICIAL NEURAL NETWORKS
Introduction & Tricks

All Rights Reserved © 2002 by Marcelo Bosque

No part of this book may be reproduced or transmitted in any form or by any means, graphic, electronic, or mechanical, including photocopying, recording, taping, or by any information storage retrieval system, without the permission in writing from the publisher.

Writers Club Press
an imprint of iUniverse, Inc.

For information address:
iUniverse, Inc.
5220 S. 16th St., Suite 200
Lincoln, NE 68512
www.iuniverse.com

ISBN: 0-595-21996-9

Printed in the United States of America

To Mary

EPIGRAPH

Life is nothing but a fight against the blindness of our misunderstandings. We are merely warriors of light, the light of knowledge facing our worst enemy: Intolerance and absence of erudition. The written word of a book is the ultimate weapon we've got to win the match.

(The author)

CONTENTS

LIST OF TABLES

PREFACE

There is a kind of magic in neural networks. Since Mary Shelley's Frankenstein times, men and women have had fantasies about life, the creation of life. In those times, a machine that could have a development like the human brain was something beyond imagination. It was easier to think in a monster made from different parts of animals and human beings. The study of intelligence and how to create it seemed to be a matter of mad scientists working at their laboratories, placed in a tower of their castle.

Nowadays, we have evolved from that *naïve* point of view: We are now serious people working at our laboratories or offices in our universities. We have studied many years in order to do that, and we spend many time creating devices that could be able to imitate the human mental resources. However, the above definition doesn't satisfy me at all. There is still a bit of Dr. Frankenstein in our souls. As he did, we still want to create something from the chaos. We feel the need to go beyond the actual knowledge, to reach the unreachable, to trespass the outer limits. In other words, I personally believe that the study of neural networks is the contemporary way that we, human beings, use to satisfy one of our deepest desires: To play God.

(The author)

ACKNOWLEDGEMENTS

This book was born by request of people. I didn't have in mind the idea of writing a book about neural networks. Everything started with a serial of articles that I published during the 1990's. In 1999 I placed them in the net in my personal page. I don't know why I did it. I really thought that very few people were going to see the work. I can't explain the magnitude of my surprise when I started to see that so many people were interested in them. Another surprise was the fact that many people were telling me they wanted more...Lots of readers suggested me in their mails that I should publish more material. Well...This book is the answer to their will.

In summary: This book is dedicated to all people who encouraged my work and gave me their support and empathy. Thank you very much indeed.

Marcelo Bosque.

LIST OF ABBREVIATIONS

The abbreviations used in this work are:

3L-BPN:	Three-Layer Back-propagation Network (= BPN)
4L-BPN:	Four-Layer Back-propagation Network
AI:	Artificial Intelligence
BPN:	One Hidden Layer Back-propagation Network
JCN:	Jump Connection Network
Nnet: or N-net:	Artificial Neural Network
OCR:	Optical Character Recognition
PHN:	Parallel hidden layers network
SAM:	Self Associative Memory Network
SOPN:	Self Organization Pattern Network

INTRODUCTION

There is a deep desire in men, in order to reproduce intelligence and place it in a machine. The fascination that this fact has made in human beings, can also be seen reflected in the appearance of a complete branch of knowledge that studies the process of intelligence. It was named "Artificial intelligence" (AI).

In the decades of 1960-1970, there was an excess of optimistic predictions about this subject. Sentences like "*In 10 years we will have a machine that could be intelligent enough to win the chess world championship*", or "*In 30 years machines will acquire the abilities of a human being*" were spread in the media. As everyone knows, XXI century came, and these predictions were far from being executed.

As a matter of fact, even though the machine called "Deep Blue" won a chess match against the world championship Mr. Kasparov in the last decade of the XX century, the machine itself is a complete "intelligent idiot". It just plays chess, but it is unable to understand or process anything else. You can see it as an ultra-sophisticated calculator machine, but no more than that. A mosquito has more intelligence than "Deep blue". In fact, I heard a sentence that says "*The match Deep Blue vs. Kasparov showed us that there is no need of intelligence to play chess*". That doesn't mean that human players are not intelligent. It means that a non-intelligent device can play chess as good as an intelligent human being.

As a result of all these facts, the credibility of artificial intelligence was hurt near to death since 1970's. In the following years, many serious scientists didn't want to get involved with projects related to AI, and it was very difficult to get research funds for this area. During the last years of the XX century, research went on, but scientists made up a wide group of speeches to mean they were working in AI, without mentioning the infamous words. Terms like "OCR" (Optical character recognition) appeared to show that someone was working in the field of printed-text computer recognition or human writing. This was one of the core matters of AI in the 1960's, but in the middle of 1980's, a serious scientist would indeed prefer to say he was performing "Research on OCR technology" than saying he was working in AI.

Other core matter of AI was the computer recognition of the human voice, the recognition of language. We have now available several programs that let you install a microphone to the computer and place what you are saying in your default word processor. These programs are not called AI programs, but "Dictation software", "Translation programs", "Keyboard- free input programs", etc. None of them present themselves as AI programs.

Nowadays, we are living a paradox:

a) We are in the AI golden age. Many of the goals that the scientists expected to get have been reached. (Scanners that read the printed text and place it in the computer, Programs that translate idioms, dictation software that let you input your speeches in the computer, robotic control programs etc.)

b) As AI was not well seen for many years, the above products were not promoted as being the result from it, so many people is unable to see the connection between them. For these people, AI is a near-to-death 1960's discipline, something old, something of the past.

c) We are far away from AI's ultimate goal: To create a machine that could be able to think. AI is still a discipline of the future.

PART I

Past, Present and Future of the Neural Networks

A NEURAL NETWORK APPEARS

One of the multiple branches of AI is the development of the "**neural networks**".

A neural network is the attempt to make inverse engineering of the brain. Classic engineering starts with a plan and then in base of it, it makes a machine or device. The inverse engineering starts with a machine and tries to understand how it works. It is the same thing as many men do at weekends in their garages when they say they will fix the old TV set.

The main idea of a neural network is that scientists try to make a computational simulation of the behavior of the human brain, reproducing in a small scale the neurons and synaptic connections of the organ.

As it is a fact that this device works in humans, the target is to try to duplicate this effect in an artificial environment.

The goal of a neural network is to reproduce the human learning mechanism and pattern recognition in a way that a computer understands.

One of the more interesting questions to be considered here is the brain ability to recognize patterns. Patterns Recognition is the ability to see a complex image (a photograph, a motion picture) and to act consequently. Digital computers were designed from a binary logic (of 2 values: 0-1 or True-False), which made their construction easier, but makes difficult to process and to recognize images, photos, planes and drawings.

Some uses of the neural networks

A small boy can watch a photo and to recognize immediately his father, himself, and the familiar pet with a 100% of effectiveness.

A computer, nevertheless, requires a lot of programming work to be able to do the same, and even so, the result if far away from the human precision.

If the computer has a pattern recognition system, it may get images of a video camera and act by itself in tasks such as recognition of personnel entrances and exits in a company (identifying people just watching the pictures captured by the video machine).

In the same way, it is simple for the human being to recognize the hand-written patterns but this task is extremely difficult for the computer.

Programs that try to get this objective are called OCR (Optical Character Recognition programs)

OCR: Definition

A OCR program consists in a software that tries to turn the digitized image of a hand-written letter into a reasonable text file that can be used by the default text processor of the computer.

An OCR program can be designed on an algorithmic base (heuristic OCR program). This type of programs are very popular at the moment, but they have an appreciable degree of inaccuracy when the copy in the piece of paper is not perfect and presents or displays " noise ", that is to say when it is not an original. (ex: a Xerox copy of a letter creates "dust" or small black dots in the copy when the original is not in excellent condition).

An OCR program based on pattern-recognition (as the neural networks) might have the ability to ignore these noise in a similar way as the human brain easily distinguishes the text and the small dots in a Xerox-copy of a hand- written letter.

In a similar way, a system based on a neural network could recognize the digitized image of a laser pulse refraction on an object and identify the quality of the painting based on that fact. Comparing the discontinuities of the captured patterns with standard patterns allows the net to find out automatically which objects have not been painted properly. If the net is connected to a robot arm with a painting injector, it is possible then to order it to repaint the piece.

Military applications also use this principle. The bounce of digitized radar that sends an airplane to its opponent is recognized by a neural network that compares the pattern with the ones of the enemy airplanes saved in its database. The aerodynamic properties and the fuselage shape of the airplane is digitalized and it is used to deduce if a enemy plane is an ally or not. The same principle is used to detect a missile launch from an earth base, comparing the pattern of the foreground with the new pattern obtained when the missile is in air. Fast information in modern wars is so important that many of the choices that were made by human beings in the past, now must be taken by the computer.

Each one of these items may deserve an individual research work. This fact gives us an idea about the amplitude of the neural network field.

Finally, it is possible to indicate that specially adaptable neural networks are suitable for scientific investigation of mathematical models with non-linear variables. In these models, the effects of the mutual interrelation of the variables make very difficult to solve them using the traditional algorithmic methods.

The brain seen from the lens of its function.

The human brain can be seen as a process (thought), that turns the inputs (mainly sensorial) into outputs (actions). A description of the symbols used can be consulted in the Appendix A. We can graphically observe this process in table RN001.

Table RN001
Process of thought considering the mind functions

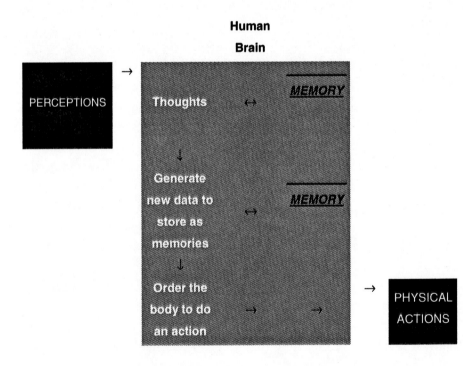

There are diverse stimuli that flows to the brain, which are called "perceptions". The human being is a system that uses sensorial inputs for his process of thought. The word "perception" includes not only the stimuli that the environment projects to the five senses but also the illusions and ideas that the own mind of the subject can discern.

The brain is stimulated by the simultaneous interrelation of perceptions, which activate the process we have called "thought". In order to do that, it is required some data, ("experiences") stored in the memory of the individual, that can be seen as a file or database called in this context "Memories ".

The process of thought has a kind of sub-product, that is the creation of data to be stored, which will be transformed as well into new memories. That implies that:

Thought is a recursive process, that uses memory both as an input and as an output. The effect of this behavior is usually called "experience"

Therefore, it is possible to see "thought" as a reading and writing process of the "*memory*" database. In the middle of these circumstances we find another sub-process: The brain has to prepare an output in the form of an order given to the body in order to do something. If the process of thought finishes with the idea *"I want to get an apple"*, the brain has to order the arm and hand to catch the apple.

This action can be physical or psychic. In the first case, determined muscles of the body are programmed to move in a defined sense.
Example: The increase of the room temperature causes in the individual the perception of heat and this directs his actions towards the ingestion of water in order to eliminate his thirst.

In the second case, a perception can take to the recovery of a memory, in other words, takes to a search in the memory database.
Example: The perception of a floral aroma causes the memory of a pleasant past experience in a field of flowers.

The brain is constituted by a vast assembly of cells called neurons, which intercommunicate to each other using electrical impulses, by means of the synaptic connections. The neurons are located in the form of a network where each one of them is a node, interlaced by means of connections that transmit electrical signals. A neuron can receive and transmit electrical signals from and towards several other neurons. Table RN002 shows this process.

Table RN002
Environment of a neuron

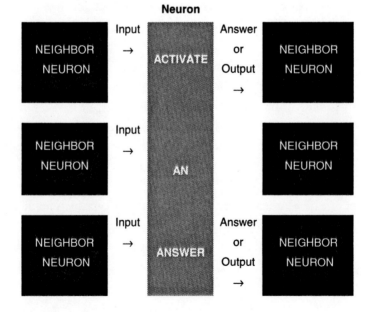

From a physical point of view, Thought consists of a series of electrical interactions between the neurons, which have the following behavior:

a) To receive Signals: Each neuron receives one or several electrical messages from the adjacent neurons.

b) To condition the unloading: The neuron acts like a transit system that takes the energy transferred to it and decides if it has to activate itself to send an answer or not.

c) To unload (To emit an answer) and to reinforce connections: The energy is expelled towards the adjacent neurons to which it is connected. At the same time, the synaptic connections are reinforced. This means that it is set up a preference system to direct the answers. The connections recently used to transmit an answer are stronger than the others, so the next time the same impulse comes to the original neuron, the output will be directed using these stronger connections.

Programming the Neuron in Pseudo-code

The AI programmers use certain techniques to be able to expose better their work. One of them is the use of the Pseudo-code. This it used to determine the logical steps that they would use independently of any computer language. The Appendix B contains pseudo-code examples so that the readers can understand it if they are not familiarized with the use of them.

The following example shows the way a neural cell works, using pseudo-code.

Pseudo code for a neural behavior

Program Neuron 1

0 DO WHILE IMPULSES OF THE NEIGHBORING NEURONS ARE RECEIVED
1 GATHER ELECTRICAL IMPULSE
2 DECIDE WHICH NEURONS WILL BE THE ELECTED ONES TO UNLOAD THE ENERGY
3
   3.1 DO WHILE THEY ARE NEURONS LEFT WITHOUT RECEIVED IMPULSE
   3.2 SELECT RECEIVING NEURON
   3.3 UNLOAD ENERGY TO THE RECEIVING NEURON
   3.4 REINFORCE CONNECTION WITH THIS NEURON
   3.5 RETURN TO POINT 3.1
4 RETURN TO BEGIN

This process continues until every neuron of the chosen ones has received its answer. In the human body, there are some neurons that are also connected with a nervous terminal, (eyes, medulla, nerves, etc.) which activate the corresponding actions.

If we examine the program, we can deduce that at any given time, there is a group of neurons that work together at the same time. (The chosen ones by the previous group of neurons). We may think of these groups as **layers** of neurons. We will have then different neuron layers that will have the function of increasing or decreasing the strength of the neural paths. (that means the probability that a certain path could be elected the next time a similar impulse excites the neuron).

These facts are coherent with brain physiology research, that agree in the existence of different specialized zones of the brain which perform the specific neural tasks.

Memory: Concept

We can say that Memory consists from this approach in the sum of strengths or preferences (called the "weights") corresponding to the connections of a layer of related neurons.

The activation of the neurons by a nervous impulse obtains as a result an emission of energy that flows through the neuron layers and cause the sensation of a " memory".

We have then that the same element (the neuron) acts like a signal driver, as memory, and as a decision manager. In computational terms we would speak of data-bus for the synaptic connection, managing software to decide when load and unloads the electric flux and ram memory , and databases and hard disk to protect the accumulated weights values.

Axioms to make able the computational simulation of the biological process

We will need some axioms in order to be able to simulate these processes by means of computational devices. Without them, the idea of an artificial neural network would have no sense.

Main axiom

We do not have to care about the physical substance which neurons are made from (DNA versus silicon). It is not important. What it counts is the function.

The neurons, like the rest of the structure of the living creatures is composed by interlaced carbon atom strings. Nevertheless, the chemical composition of the same ones is not a determining factor at the time of trying to duplicate them. The important point is the function, not the raw material. If we believe in this axiom, we can conclude that it is possible to create an artificial neuron simulating its functions in an artificial (non human) device like a computer. If we do not use this assumption, the study of artificial neural networks would have to be suspended since it would not be possible to make them.

This axiom takes us to think about brain webs like a kind of " carbon networks ". Some of their functions can be simulated by devices created in another material.

A wheel can be done in wood, metal or vulcanized rubber, but it is always a wheel.

Secondary axiom

The " intelligent " behavior (limited in this case the recognition of patterns) is done by the interrelation of messages and interactions of the network nodes.

This means that if we have an artificial substitute of the neurons, and we apply between them a similar mechanism of interaction to the used by the human brain, some of the abstract brain functions will be duplicated or simulated.

If we do not have this axiom, it wouldn't either be possible to continue with the Nnet research since there wouldn't be a way to reproduce the behavior using artificial neurons.

Considering the existence of the enunciated theorems, we should define now the computational equivalence of the elements seen previously.

Table RN003 shows to equivalence between the artificial elements and the biological ones in order to reproduce a neuronal layer:

TABLE RN003
Artificial equivalent of biological elements

BIOLOGICAL ELEMENT	ARTIFICIAL ELEMENT
NEURON	**Network node =**
	Ram memory +
	Hard Disk space +
	Neural network software
Sensorial Input	Digital Images and signals
	Computer Files
BEHAVIOR (SENSORIAL OUTPUT)	Creation of computer files containing the output data
	Execution of a pre-defined computer program
	Activation of robotic interfaces
Synaptic Connections	Transferences between the memory positions.
	Values and weights of the data passed from node to node

PART II

Steps to execute a Neural Network

STEPS TO EXECUTE A NEURAL NETWORK

The artificial process consists in the creation of a computer program (software) that could be able to:

- Capture digitalized data
- Generate memory spaces. This can be done by the creation of multiple memory arrays.
- Give an order of preference or "weight" symbolizing this way the different strengths between layers from neurons
- Assign to the first array the status of input layer, which will contain then the captured digitalized data.
- Assign to the last array the status of output layer, allowing that its values could be transformed by the interaction of the other elements of the network
- Assign to the intermediate layers the status of hidden layers, allowing that their values could be modified by the interaction of the other elements of the network.
- Forward Propagation: To make operations of transference between the data of the layers simulating this way the synaptic interconnections.
- Collect the output layer values, which will be taken as the network value for a given input value.
- Once obtained the output network value, to assign an action depending on it. (Ex: The creation of an information file, or the activation of an automatic robot device)

Step 1 Getting the Digitalized Data

The neural network must start with the artificial equivalent of a stimulus to be able to operate. In a living organism the stimulation is done by the excitation of any of the senses or a combination of the excitation of several of them.

In the computer, this process must be divided in two parts:

1 The neural network program must be opened, it requires an external human activation to work. This is an automatic task in the living beings.
2 Requires an input (a pattern to recognize).

Any input must be turned to digital format to be able to be transformed into a file susceptible to be understood by the computer.

To digitalize information we must transform the input data into a zero-one string, which is called a "binary string". This string must be stored in a file or database that keeps the information. In general, we can use a vector or array, in order to increase the speed of the process. (An array locates the patterns in RAM, so the data search is faster than a database location). As we have seen, the data is grouped into layers in the net, so we can say that the input pattern can be seen as the input layer. That's why the vector is named " **Input Layer** ".

Example of Input layer:

Let's suppose that we want to make an OCR neural Network. We've got a scanner that digitalizes text of books and we want a net that could be able to recognize the patterns and convert them into letters and numbers in order to place them in a text file. The scanner reads the piece of paper and generate a graphic file as the result. (A .GIF or .JPG graphic file containing a shape that represents the number one). Suppose we place in the scanner a piece of paper with just this shape:

Shape 1

1

A human being (In our terms we can speak about a *carbon neural network*) recognizes that this is the number one in less than a second. The computer just see a symbol. Remember that we have NOT pressed the "1" key in the keyboard. The machine has only got a graphic file with a shape in it. The target is to make the computer recognize it as the number one.

The composition of a graphic file is a serial of dark dots and white dots. When the dots are put closely, they simulate to be solid shapes. We will use the term pixels to call the dots. Each pixel has a color attached to it. So, we can say that the graphic file is a string of white and black pixels. The "noise" in the scanned pieces of paper is constituted by errors of scanning, where a white pixel is seen as a black one.

If we separate a bit the pixels from the file, the shape would look like this:

Shape 2

```
_ _ ¦ _ _
_ ¦ ¦ _ _
_ _ ¦ _ _
_ _ ¦ _ _
_ ¦ ¦ _ _
```

Shape 2 is the same image as shape 1. The only difference is that the pixels have been separated a bit to show each one by its own.

In order to work with a neural network, the graphic file must be converted into a binary string.

To complete it, the white pixels must be replaced by a "0" and each black string can be replaced by a "1". So our shape becomes:

Shape 3
0 0 **1** 0 0
0 **1** **1** 0 0
0 0 **1** 0 0
0 0 **1** 0 0
0 **1** **1** 0 0

If we show the same data in a binary string format, (Row1+ Row2+ Row3 etc.) we will have:

String 1
0,0, **1**, 0, 0 ,0, **1**, **1**, 0 ,0 ,0 ,0 **1**, 0, 0 ,0 ,0 , **1**, 0, 0 ,0 , **1**, **1**, 0, 0

String1 is now a proper data format to constitute the input layer, so the input layer for shape 1 (the initial shape) is:

Input Layer 1
0,0, **1**, 0, 0 ,0, **1**, **1**, 0 ,0 ,0 ,0 **1**, 0, 0 ,0 ,0 , **1**, 0, 0 ,0 , **1**, **1**, 0, 0

In summary: The neural network must transform any input from the capture devices (as scanners) into binary strings, in order to work with them.

The reader who wishes to continue investigating on this subject will find in the Appendix C summary information relative to data digitalization.

Step 2 Generation of memory space

One of the forms to simulate artificially neurons is to assimilate them to elements of arrays or vectors. Any programming language offers the possibility to create n - dimensional arrays. The amount of arrays depends on the architecture of the network to choose. The selection of the ideal architecture requires a detailed analysis that exceeds to the magnitude of this work in special. The interested reader can find greater information on this subject in the Annexed E " Network architectures". This work has been made thinking about the architecture of a "One Hidden Layer Back-propagation Network" or **BPN with one hidden layer**.

The initial number of arrays involved will be then:

I) One array to store the input layer whose number of elements agrees with the number of elements of this layer. See Equation 1 at Table RN004 in order to see the mathematics of this item.

II) One array to store the hidden layer of variable size (with the same size of the input layer).

III) One array to store the output layer with a variable number of elements according to the number of outputs that must have the network.

In this step the arrays are usually filled with nil values, generally zeros. See the mathematical equation for this step at table RN004, point 3 at the bottom of this section.

Step 3 Set order of preference or weight for the neural layers

As it has been explained in preceding paragraphs, the network tries to simulate the energy movement in the synaptic interconnection, reinforcing (weighing) the frequent connections.

This is obtained annexing to each value of the layer a random value called **weight** in the specific vocabulary. The weights are then values, which are multiplied by the new values of the layers to obtain the outputs or results that are transferred from one layer to the following one.
See the mathematical equation for this step at table RN004, point 4 at the bottom of this section.

The function of the weights is to recognize and separate one pattern from another. **The weights must be settle down a priori of the effective execution of the network by a process called " training ".**

In other words: Once the network software has been developed, and before the N-net is ready to work, the operator must "train" the software in order to make it recognize the patterns. **A neural network is a software that learns, but this learning must be done before the execution.** Once the network was trained, a new set of weights are made, which can be saved in a database. When the network is required to work, it only has to call these values saved in the database and load them as weights values.

The network will need then:

IV) One array to store the input-layer weights. This array will have the same number of elements as the input layer and will have as well stored the relative strengths to each pattern that the network can recognize, reason why it must be a two-dimension array.

Example:

If the input layer has 1000 elements and the network can recognize 8 different patterns, the array will have one first dimension of 1000 and one second dimension of 8. If we want to program this array in a computer, in Visual Basic or ASP languages, we should place: DIM WEIGHTS (1000,8)

See the mathematical equation for this step at table RN004, point 5 at the bottom of this section.

V) One array to store the hidden layer weights to the output layer

This array must contain at least the same elements as the output array

Step 4 Set up the first array (the one with the pattern data) as the "input layer".

As it is said before, the values taken from a capture device are supposed to be placed in a database. These values must be converted in a binary string, and entered in the "input layer" array.

The network can load the initial data from just a database or a combined set of a data-entry device and a database. The first option means that there are some external input devices that capture the patterns and place them in a database, which is used by the network in order to input the data.

The second option is: If the data-entry device is integrated to the neural network, it can capture the input layer data and transfer it to the net, so the input database is just needed for weights and the output data.

These capture devices can be:

Usual capture devices:

- Human operator
- Internet Connection
- E-mail
- Digital camera
- video Camera
- Scanner
- Digital prints reader
- Sound recorder / microphone
- Web-cam

Step 5: Set up the last array as the "output layer"

If the network was already trained and configured, there must be a database with the output values previously entered. In this point, the output layer array is loaded with the output values taken from the database.

Step 6: Set up the middle arrays as "hidden layers"

The values of the hidden layers will be transformed by the interaction of the other elements of the net. This process must be repeated for all the hidden layers. In the default example of this book, there is a 1 hidden layer network, so we'll have just one hidden layer, but other architectures may use two or more ones.

Step 7: Forward Propagation

The Forward propagation is a way used to simulate the synaptic interconnection process. The data are transferred from one array to the next one, simulating the neural flow of electric impulses. This transference is called "propagation". In the case of forward propagation the flow follows the natural order, from the input layer to the output layer. The opposite is the backpropagation, where the data flows from the output layer to the input layer.

In the forward propagation, having the pattern entered in the input layer and the weights for the input layer, the net calculates the hidden layer values for that input layer. With those values of the hidden layer, and having the weights for the hidden layer, the net calculates then the output layer values for that input pattern and loads them in the "output layer" array of the network.

In summary: The forward propagations starts with the input layer value and calculates the outputs for that patterns.

Mathematical Equations of the neural Network

The object of this book is to present the subject as simple as possible. That's why I have tried to explain how the nets work without using any mathematics at all. In general, all the works I have read use a lot of mathematics in order to explain the concepts. I suppose that this practice makes the book a more erudite work, but has a disadvantage: It makes them impossible to read from ordinary people, (or at least people who want to read about N-nets and doesn't have a PhD in mathematics). However, if there are people interested in the practical mathematic concepts beyond the neural networks, here I place a table that contains the core equations implied in the development of a N-net. People who dislike mathematics may simple go to Part III of this book. Table RN004 shows the mathematical concepts implied in a N-net.

Table RN 004
Mathematical Equations of the neural Network

Description	Equation
In Step 2 **"Generation of memory space"** we must create one array to store the input layer whose number of elements agrees with the number of elements of this layer.	Equation 1 $E = (e1..en)$
We must also create one array to store the hidden layer whose number of elements agrees with the number of elements of this layer.	Equation 2 $\Pi = (h1..hn)$
The third step is to create one array to store the output layer with a variable number of elements according to the number of outputs that must have the network.	Equation 3 $\Omega = (s1..sn)$
The weights values, are multiplied by the new values of the layers to obtain the outputs	Equation 4 $$\Omega_{(n)} = \sum_{l=1}^{n} \Pi(h1..h_n) * E(e1..en)$$
One array is created to store the input-layer weights	Equation 5 $T(x, y) = (x1..x_n, y1..y_n)$
One array to store the hidden layer weights to the output layer	Equation 6 $\Delta = (p1..pn)$

26

PART III

Forward Propagation

FORWARD PROPAGATION

To calculate the values in order to propagate one layer to the next one we must start with the values of the current layer. Then, we must apply the chosen **activation function** to the data. In this point we are able to multiply it by the respective weights.

An activation function is a mathematical function that is applied to the untouched data and returns a result that is able to be multiplied by the proper weights in order to generate the input for the next layer. This weight simulates the strength or weakness of the synaptic connection between the neurons. When the value of the associated weight is important, we have the simulation of a strong connection. When it is irrelevant we will have a weak connection. A weight with zero value means a null connection. In other words: $\text{Layer}_1 = \text{Layer}_0$ x activation function x weights

Another way of saying the same is:
$y = f(x)$
activation function output= $f(\text{Layer}_0)$
$\text{Layer}_1 = $ Activation function (Layer_0) x weights

In our default example of a one hidden-layer network we'll have that:

Input Layer= Conversion of the captured pattern into a binary string
Hidden Layer= Activation function(**Input Layer**) x input-layer weights
Output Layer= Activation function(**Hidden Layer**) x hidden-layer weights

When the network finds an answer, forward propagation is completed.

Election of an Activation Function:

If the chosen activation function were the hyperbolic tangent, we could then have: $f(x)=tanh(x)$

The election of an adequate activation function is a craftsman choice from the network designer that places a trace of its own personal touch. Two different networks made for the same purpose will differ from each other in the election of their activation functions. This fact gives the activation functions the status of "signature" or "personal touch" of the designer. Some of them uses the function in order to convert the data into normalized serials, as could be the use of the sigmoid or sinus functions. Some others apply elaborated hand-made functions.

Readers can find more information about activation functions in Appendix D.

Step 8: Collect the value of the output layer

This value will be the result from the net search. The value can be stored in a memory variable or saved in a database field for its later use. Some nets convert the result to another format before saving it, because in general the raw result is a number. If the net uses a database with these numbers associated with proper descriptions, then the final answer could be a description instead of a number.

Step 9: Set up the actions attached to the network output

The network output can be attached to another computer program. This second program could be executed once the net reaches its answer.

In this case, the net commands the way the program is executed and it sets up the behavior of the second program.

The actions that can take a program in base to the network output can be:

- Informative: The program informs that an answer for the input pattern has been found. Example: In a network designed to classify different sizes of bottles, the net uses as input the digital image taken from a video camera. The camera focuses the production line in which several sizes of bottles are circulating. The net has to recognize any size different to the standard ones and report this fact to the operator. The network input is then the digital image taken from the camera, and the output is the identification of the size of the bottle. An informative action could be the execution of a warning message on screen each time that a bizarre bottle is found.

- Operative: In this case, after the warning message, the program executes some procedure. If we continue with the example of the bottle classification, we could have an operative action if the program is attached to a robotic arm control, and it orders the arm to extract the bizarre bottle from the production line. As al alternate procedure, the computer could open a trap-door in the production line and let the bottle fall down into a waste basket.

- Predictive: In this case the program uses the network output to forecast the behavior of a variable. Example: A network with weather data as an input patterns could be used to make predictions about the future weather and then spread this information to the proper government agencies.

Using again the pseudo-code to make an example, it is possible to have a first approximation to a neural network.

Program Neural Network 1

	PROGRAM NEURAL NETWORK 1	
0	Start Program	
1	Dimension Arrays (Depending on the network architecture)	
2	Name the first array "Input Layer"	
3	Name the last array "Output Layer"	
4	Name the intermediate arrays "Hidden Layers"	
5	5.1 if exists a file or database with input patterns then	
		5.2 read values and store them in the input-layer array
	5.3 else	
	5.4 end program	
6	6.1 if exists a file or database with input-layer weights then	
		6.2 read values and store them in the input-layer weights array
	6.3 else	
	6.4 end program	
7	7.1 if exists a file or database with output patterns then	
		7.2 read values and store them in the output layer array
	7.3 else	
	7.4 end program	
8	Do while exists hidden layers	
		8.1 Get values from the previous layer
		8.2 Calculate values emerging from the activation function
		8.3 Multiply these values by the weights of the layer
		8.4 Send the results to the next layer
	8.5 if this is the last layer then	
		8.6 Send results to the output layer
	8.7 loop until there are no more hidden layers	
9	Read output layer values	
10	Seek in the output description database the meaning in words of the output values	
11	Send report to the network operator using the meaning of the output values	
12	Execute the default program for the output value	
	End network	

Table RN004 shows the first level of the execution of a Neural Network main program.

Table RN004.

Neural Network Execution (Main program)

Training the neuronal network: Weights of the neuron layers

In step 3 it has been exposed that weights layers must be " trained " before they are able to recognize the patterns, (this process is equivalent to the " memory" of the human brain).

To train the network means that we must place the proper weights in the net in order to let it be able to connect a specific input pattern with a specific output answer. This process is equivalent to increase or to attenuate the synaptic connections between the neurons.

Getting suitable weights:

As it has been said previously, this procedure varies according with the network architecture we are using and the programmer design of it. Therefore, the following paragraphs must be taken as merely examples. They do no show all the possibilities that can be used.

One of the usual methods consist in determining the weights according to some error-minimization algorithm. These algorithms are designed as a recursive process where the network designer:

- Loads a sample input layer and expected output

The designer introduces a sample pattern to the network and its expected output value. This means that the network must be trained in order to get "1" as the result of this specific binary string.

Example: Going back to a previous example where we worked with the pattern of number "1". We finished it with the following pattern, that is the binary string corresponding to the digital pattern of a letter that contains only the "1" written.

Input Layer 1
0, 1, 0, 1, 1, 0, 0, 1, 0, 0, 1, 0, 0, 1, 0, 0, 1, 0

Gives the weights initial values (generally random values)
Input Layer Weights

0, 0, 1, 0, 1, 0, 1, 1, 0, 1, 1, 0, 1, 1, 0, 0, 1, 1

This is a randomly selected string. It has no meaning at this moment.

- Runs the net using these weights. As the net is not trained, the output value will not be "1". The real output will not be equal to the expected value. There are many ways of working with these values. We will name **error** to the difference between the expected output value and the real output value of the network. However, this is only one of the possible measurement systems. When we talk about methods that minimize the error, it is very common to talk about the "Delta Rule", for example, that says the error is: *error = (Expected Output–Net output) * Net output * (1–Net output).*

- Measures the resulting error: The measurement in itself is an artisan process that can be done in many ways. As it is said in the previous paragraph, in the present book the error will be taken as the difference between of the network output and its expected output value. So, for us, we'll have that:

Error=Expected Output-Network Output

- Determinates the error trend: The designer changes the weights in a given direction (increasing or decreasing the values in a small percentage) and executes again the network. If the new error diminishes, the tendency is towards the error minimization of the error. In opposite case the tendency must be reverted. Once that the trend is determined, the designer chooses the minimum error that the net must accept to work properly. This is a given value and depends on the exactitude that is required in the pattern recognition. Example: The designer may say "The network must have an error of 0,05% or less".

- Executes an iterative process where the weights are varied following the trend direction. Each new serial of values are then stored as the new weights. This process continues until the error is smaller or equal to the expected minimum error.

At this point the weight values are stored in the database. The net is trained to recognize this specific pattern.

This procedure must be repeated for each pattern. In other words, the net has to be trained for every pattern that it has to recognize. When a new pattern appears, the net has to be retrain again. The training of the network is assimilated to the learning process in a human being.

As a new layer is entered, an iterative process is necessary where the old patterns must be reintroduced again, to avoid that the old associated weights could be lost. In a human being, we could say that each time a new knowledge is given to the net, the old knowledge may be forgotten, so the old knowledge must be reinforced. The new weights must be able to recognize not only the new patterns but also the old ones.

The final weight values are then stored in the weights database to serve as input weight values for the execution of the neural network. In this point it is said that the network is already trained, reason why is qualified for the recognition of patterns. Anyway, the net will only recognize those patterns who are similar to the given trained ones.

Final steps

The network sends a message to the operator informing that the training has finished and that it is ready to be executed.
The operator may execute the network at that moment or keep the weights in the corresponding file for later use. The training can be done by the network operator previously to execution (for example at the end of the previous day) or just in time. As it may consume much time, it is recommended the first alternative. Table RN005 shows the Diagram of the training process of the network.

Table RN005
Neural Network Training System

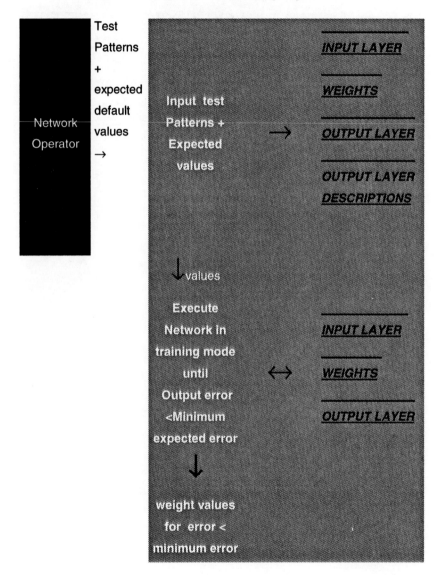

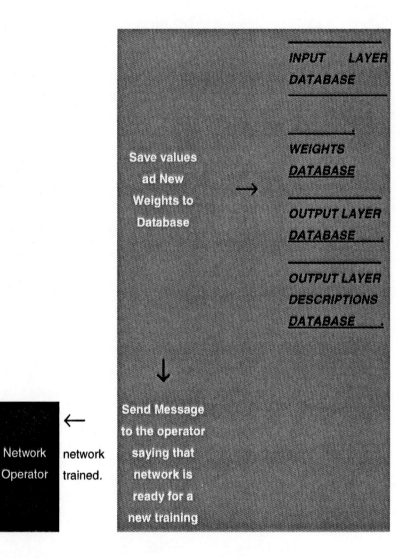

PART IV

Programming a neural Network

Methodology and samples to program a Neural Network

The idea of this section is to give help and tricks to the readers who might want to make their own nets.

I have read many books about N-nets, and one of the failures that in general they got is that they don't tell you how to do it. In general, they explain the research work that the author has done, and other related themes, but they don't care about the people who are reading the book. In general, the language is extremely cryptic and confusing and the authors tell what they've done, not *how* they did it.

When I started to program N-nets, I had a lot of failures and mistakes. In this section I'd like to talk about them and tell the readers the tricks I have discovered during that process. Perhaps calling it a "Methodology" sounds too arrogant, but that's what it is. Is the way, the steps that I use to do it, now that I've got some years of experience doing it. These steps came into light after years of practical proofs on the field, and I expect that could be able to save you hours (or days) of worthless work.

One of the main concepts I'd like to say is that as far as I'm concerned, a neural network can be programmed in any modern computer language.

In ancient times, AI languages like Lisp or Prolog were used in an exclusive way. It was supposed that if you were doing something related with

AI, then you should write your code either in Lisp or Prolog. The use of Lisp was preferred in America and Prolog in Europe.

I have used both many years ago when I was learning about AI, and I discovered that their functions could easily be emulated in any computer language if you know how to do it. The logic inference motor of them does not guarantee you at all to have a better performance than a modern Object-oriented language. As a matter of fact, I've never liked to be a prisoner of any computer environment, so I prefer to use the tools I like best. Nowadays we can feel free to use the technology we like. I personally prefer the Java-Script/Java environment or the VB-Script / ASP one because they were designed for Internet and they give instant access to the Web. However, these samples have been developed using Visual Basic ™ , because is a very well known and popular language, and my objective is that my work could be able to be understood by as many readers as possible.

As it was said before, the most popular N-net architecture is the Back - propagation Network . In this section a three layer BPN will be programmed using the Visual Basic language.

Steps to create a Neural Network

Step 1: Define the environment

First of all, we will need a name for our project. We can call it "BPN" project.

Then we will need a database in order to store the data. ASP/Visual Basic environment accepts SQL Server or Access databases.

Many authors say that SQL server databases are the best, but I personally didn't have any trouble with Access databases. (I have used very large files in my life). I don't know if the ones who claim for SQL really mean that or if they are supporting the marketing effort of SQL's vendors. It is not the goal of this book to discuss which one is better. You may choose the one you like best.

Let's remember that the net has to be connected in some way with a captured device like a scanner or a video camera. This device must capture the pattern, digitalize it and place the binary string in a file. We will need then a program or person that fills the permanent storage tables with these patterns. (In other word someone who to copy and paste the strings into the database) As this is just a secondary operation, we will assume that this operation has been already done.

So, at this point, we've got a database with the BPN-original table filled with the patterns we want the net to recognize. A real-life professional network may have patterns of 100000-1000000 (or more) elements. If we consider that each pixel of a graphic file is an element, a file of 200K contains more than 200000 pixels. This excessive number of items makes the net to run extremely slowly if you are not using a mainframe.

However, the network design and architecture are the same, independently of the number of items of the patterns. That's why in this book we'll focus on the network architecture and we will use small sample patterns to work with. They make the network run faster and does not interfere with the way it is made.

In summary: The BPN sample network will work with an Access database that will need to have these tables:

Step 2 Define the Data Structure

Our data will be located as tables in our database, each one containing fields where the data will be placed.

Trick: It is useful to use permanent data tables and temporal data tables.

Step 2.1: Permanent storage tables

a) BPN-original . To store all input patterns.

It contains the fields: *Layer-number, row, column, value, pattern-code-name*
We can put the pattern number in the columns (for example) and the pattern items in the rows.

Example: Suppose we have three strings:

1) "000111000" corresponding to "Shape1"
2) "000000111" corresponding to "Shape2"
3) "111000000" corresponding to "Shape3"

Each string has 9 elements, so we've got three patterns of three items. If we design "1" to the input layer, our first record of the table would be:

Layer-number: 1
Row: 1 (First element)
Column: 1 (First string)
Value: 0 (the first element of the first string has value 0)
Pattern-name: Shape1 (The name of the first string)

In other words: we will have a table with 27 records (3 shapes x 9 elements)

b) BPN-weights-original. To store all weights. It contains the same structure as BPN-Original. In the beginning, the net is not trained, so the table is filled with random values. Once the net is trained, the values make the input pattern be recognized. These values are stored here. If the weighs values weren't stored, we would have to train it each time the net has to be run. (The training is a very time-consuming process). It is a good idea to save the weighs values in a permanent table apart from the actual work table. Sometimes, when we are training the network a new input pattern degrades the performance of the weights and it is not unusual that we would like to go back to try again. In those moments we need an original (untouched) version of the weights. That's why I have created two tables: this one and a second one called BPN-weights that is just used to work with the actual pattern.

Trick: Many N-nets just return an insipid value like "0.123456". This says nothing for the user. It is useful to have a "targets" table where the net should seek to have an answer like "The pattern correspond to a B2 Stealth Bomber Airplane"

c) **Targets-original.** To store all target values. It contains three fields: Target-number, target-name and target-value.
Example: If we have three possible answers, our first record of the table would be:

Target-number: 1
Target-name: *"Centered pattern"* (Name of the element)
Target-value: 0,9

This means that if the network processes an input pattern and it calculates a value of 0,9 for it, the net has to answer that the pattern is a "Centered pattern", or whatever we place as a target-name. If the patterns correspond to military airplane shapes, a target name could be *"F14 Tomcat"*.

Step 2.2: Temporary Working tables

(Temporary tables just to work in a single network search)
Data 1: **BPN**. To store the input pattern we are working with. It has the same structure as BPN-Original.

Data 2: **BPN-weights**. To store the weights we are working with. It has the same structure as BPN-weights-Original.

Data3: **Targets**. To store target values we are working with. It has the same structure as Targets-Original.

Step 3: Define Environmental variables

As any system, the network will need some variables to work properly. In Visual Basic, we've got the "main" form to work. We can use text objects to place the variables. We will have eight variables, so we'll need eight objects: Text1 to Text8 to store temporary values. The property **.text** of a text object let us change the object's value.

Example:
Text1.Text= ""   'reserved for later use
Text2.Text = 9   *'maximum size of each pattern*
Text3.Text = 8   *'total number of patterns stored in the database*
Text4.Text = 3   'hidden *weight layer size*
Text5.Text = 6   'current pattern number
Text6.Text = 0.025   'minimum acceptable error
Text7.Text = 1000   'number of iterations before finish training
Text8.Text = 0.5   'learning speed

Maximum Pattern size:

When the net loads the inputs, it counts the size of each one and puts in this variable the maximum length. (The number of elements that has each pattern). It is very important that all the strings may have the same number of elements. If some ones have few items, the difference must be filled with "0" values. It depends on the network and the hardware environment the maximum pattern size allowed. If the N-net operator discovers that the performance slows dramatically beyond some number of items per string, then this value must be setup as a limit and the net architecture has to be changed if necessary.

Total number of patterns:

Its meaning vary upon the use of the network. In a N-net that recognizes military airplane shapes, the number of patterns mean the quantity of planes that the net can detect. The N-net may also extract this value from the database counting the records stored. In general, N-nets work properly with a small number of strings and their performance start to decay beyond some point. We can add more length to the hidden layers in order to increase the number of shapes, but this has an exponential effect on the net speed. It is worthless to have a net that distinguishes all the shapes required, but that is so slow that the people do not want to use it. When these cases happen, the network operator might think seriously in using another architecture like a PHN, that has parallel hidden layers, each one with its own weights, so the number of shapes may be increased proportionally to the number of hidden layers.

Hidden Weight Layer size:

The hidden layer can have a user-sizeable length. The effect that a longer weight layer may cause in terms of effectiveness must be seen in each case. Not always a bigger hidden layer means a better recognition system , but in general a heavier hidden layer means a poor and slowly N-net.

Current Pattern number:

When we train the network, we must use all of the database patterns. This variable shows the actual pattern number we are using. If we are just executing the net, it shows the number of the pattern recognized.

Minimum acceptable error:

This is useful only in the training process. A 0.0025 value means an acceptable error of 0,25%. The network operator must identify the tolerance of the N-net recognition, in terms of the percentage of error it may admit. This concept must be understood properly: If we increase the error value, the net will be able to recognize "similar" shapes to the one stored in the database. If we input an airplane image whose shape is similar to the one stored, the net will recognize it anyway. However, the net will also be able to identify false shapes as a valid one. A large bird or a delta-wing could be recognized as an airplane, for example.

Trick: Make several proofs with different error values in order to calibrate the network in such a way that it may be able to recognize the correct patterns.

Number of iterations before the training finishes:

Trick: Use an iteration counter in your net to prevent that the training processes may become too slow.

This is a variable that the experience has taught me to use. When we use the above method of the minimum error to train the N-net, we are saying to it:

"Run the training algorithm until the error is equal or less than the minimum error"

This is the standard method to train the net. However, I have seen that some nets may delay hours or days doing it. If the programmer detects that the net is spending too much time to be trained, we can put a safety clause that says:

"Stop training if more than 1000 iterations have been made and the error is still bigger than the minimum expected one".

In these cases, I have seen that it is useful to reconsider the environment variables or some of the network architecture in order to setup it in a more synchronic way with the reality. Perhaps we are using patterns that are too similar and we must think about diversity. Perhaps the patterns are too big and the net uses too much time calculating. We might see the possibility to use shorter strings and see the results.

In DNA pattern recognition, only less than 1% of the pattern is used, because the DNA molecule is so big that it is nearly impossible to work with all of it.

Learning speed:

This is a variable that takes control of the network learning. The net can be configured to learn very fast the new patterns, but this action has a risk. If the process is too fast, the net will forget the old strings of its memory. In order to acquire a new pattern without forgetting the old ones,

Trick: It is advisable to setup an intermediate learning speed for the net.

Step 4: Define Main Functions

We have to remember that we have two processes, that can be done by the same program or by different ones:
   a) Training of the N-net
   b) Running (Search of data) of the net

We must train the net to get the right weights for the patterns, each time we add a new shape to the net database, but once we have made it, we just use it. That means we run the net in order to let it recognize the input pattern.

If we have two separate modules, one for training and one for running, then the main function of a BPN for running must:

a) Setup the tables, load the input data and the weighs into the net, and give initial values to the environment variables
b) Make a forward propagation of the input pattern
c) Get the output value for that input
d) Display a message to the operator telling the value

A main function in Visual Basic would look like this:

Function bpn(bpnpattern)

'BPN for Running only. No training

st=setup-tables()

if st=true then

forwardpropagate(bpnpattern)
bpn=getoutput()
MsgBox "Output of pattern " & Str(bpnpattern) & " is: " & Str(bpn)

End if
End Function

If we prefer to make the net train the weights, then the main function would be:

Function bpn2(bpnpattern, limit)

'BPN execution complete. Includes training

Do While Net-Error > limit
Setup-tables()
forwardpropagate(bpnpattern)   'requires pattern number

calc-output-error (Text4.Text)
adjust-weights()
Loop
Bpn2="Network Trained for pattern: & str(bpnpattern)
End function

This are just examples of a main function. The complete source code may be found at Appendix F **"Source code for a sample Neural Network"**.

EPILOGUE

The neural networks study offers a field of useful investigation to those people interested in creating computational models that could execute " intelligent " functions, that previously were limited to humans. As new models and architectures are developed, neural networks are expected to be able to help people with their daily process of existence. The author hopes that the data and concepts spilled in this work could give the profane reader a brief reference of the subject.

The language and terms used in this book have tried to be accessible to the ordinary people, although the complexity of the subject takes to the use of many specific words related to the neural network world.

CONCLUSIONS

Where are we now?

What have we learnt from all of this?

The study of the neural networks shows us a paradox:

First of all, we can say that many goals have been reached in this fields. N-nets are a reality today. Many of them are already working around the world and they are being used for many topics. Very well-known enterprises claim that they use neural networks' based systems to improve their operative performance.

However, the theme is still widely unknown. At the moment, all we can do with the neural networks is to make them recognize few specific patterns. If a net recognizes people's faces, for example, it is not able to recognize animal's shapes as well.

In the other hand we've got the human brain, that is an all-purpose pattern recognition system. Any human being is able to recognize hundreds of shapes and patterns every day. We do it all the time and very fast!
At the moment I am writing this, I've got in my desk a computer, a keyboard, a mouse, a plastic glass, a spoon, a sugar pot, etc. All of these things are shapes, patterns that I have recognized using my biological neural network. I did it in just a second, as everybody can do it. A two-years' old child can do it.

However, the strongest artificial neural network made up to now is far away from doing something similar.

In conclusion: The ultimate goal about neural networks is still to come. N-nets are a field of the future. We've got more research to do. The field of study is very far away from being completed.

As a matter of fact, it is opened for every researcher interested in it. We are still raiders of the lost arc, searching for the sacred grail of technology. An artificial machine that could be able to think, a Dr. Frankenstein's monster of real life is still a promise to come.

ABOUT THE AUTHOR

Dr. Marcelo Bosque (L.A.) is graduated from U.B.A. (University of Buenos Aires) and teaches the grade subject "Information Technology" at it. He has done many research works in the field of Artificial Intelligence.

Some of them are:

- Expert Systems (1992)
- Expert Systems for Forecasting Financial Analysis (1993)
- Expert Systems for Visual Languages (1995)
- Optimization methods based on Genetic Algorithms (1996)

During 1998 he wrote a serial of articles about Neural networks that were compiled and published in his personal Web Site. The positive effect and good response of the readers encouraged him to revise them and to perform a more complete approach to this subject. This book is the result of his research.

APPENDIX A

Symbols and procedures used to Diagram Data Flows

I haven't seen a specially developed model to show data-flow diagrams of the neural network processes. That's why I have created my own one. The idea was to make something easy to understand, with few elements and easy to write. I have chosen to use very simple shapes and a black & white environment in order to be able to write the symbols with just a word processor. My symbols do not need a special graphic design software to be made.

The graphic elements to be represented can be divided into background and foreground symbols: The basic background symbols can be seen in the table A1.1

Table A1.1
Basic Background Symbols

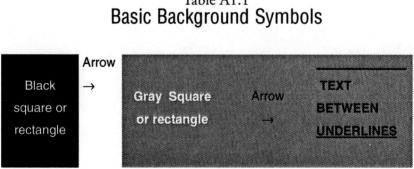

The background symbols represent the environment of the neural network. Over them are placed the actions that have to be executed in order to run the net.

- A gray square or rectangle represents the network itself: It can also be called "the network" or "the net". It determinates the net limits. The net itself is not the only device (as it could seem), because it needs to have interaction with humans and capture devices (for example), that are not part of the it, but are needed to let it work. In other words: If a symbol is placed inside the gray rectangle, that means it belongs to the network itself. If a symbol is outside the gray rectangle, then it is not part of the core network.
- A Black square or rectangle represent the space of a input-output device or a network operator.
- A text between lines represents a file or a database.
- An arrow represents a data flow. It can be a single-headed arrow or a double-headed arrow

When we join the background shapes with their meanings, we've got the foreground symbols. Table A1.2 shows the basic foreground symbols.

Table A1.2
Basic Foreground Symbols

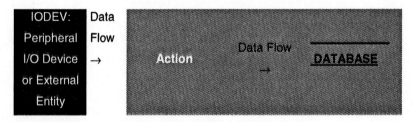

- **IODEVs: Peripheral input/output devices:** Also called External Beings or entities: An Iodev can be a human being or a machine. They provide information or they collect the network outputs, and the network needs them in order to get the input patterns, but they are not part of the network itself. Any capture device as a scanner or digital camera attached to the net are Iodevs. It is also an Iodev the net designer who gets the reports given by the network. The information required can be provided in several formats. It can be a piece of paper , a diskette, a CD - ROM, an e - mail etc.

- **Actions:** Also called Processes: An action is a technical word used here to expose the activities, the steps that the network has to do in order to transform an input into an output. If we speak about the programming language in which the net was made, the actions are the procedures and functions of the net. The typical actions are made to manipulate the network data. Typical actions are: Data Input, deletion, browse and edition.

- **Data Flows:** When an arrow comes from or goes to a file or database, that means a reading/writing operation in it. The data is stored or retrieved from the database. If the arrow enters or exits the gray rectangle, that means we are in front of an input or output operation with this data. The double-headed arrow is used to represent a reading and writing operation in a database. Some data is read, and some other is saved to the file.

- **Databases:** As we talked many times in this book, input layers, weights, outputs and some other data must be stored somewhere for later use when needed. To store them permanently, a database is generally used. However, it is very common to work with computer arrays while the net runs, because they are faster than a database. The symbol does not differentiate between one an the other. It depends on the net designer to use one or the other.

The generic interpretation of a diagram could be seen then in table A1.2

Table A1.2
Generic interpretation of the Neural Networks Data flow diagram

Iodev 1	**Data Flow1** →	**Action 1**	**Data Flow2** →	**DATABASE1**	
		↓data flow 3			
Iodev 2	**Data Flow4** →	**Action 2**	**Data Flow5** →	**DATABASE2**	
		↓data flow 6			
Iodev 3	**Data Flow7** →	**Action 3**			
		↓data flow 8			
Iodev 4	**Data Flow10** ←	**Action 4**	**Data Flow9** ←	**DATABASE3**	

Appendix B

Introduction to the use of pseudo-code:

The use of pseudo-code to narrate complex processes is widely known in technical literature. It is used to simulate a computer program without writing real code. It is very useful, because it explains the computer logic, but let the readers use their favorite computer language, at the same time.

The first step in order to make a computer program is to divide the problem in a series of actions or simple steps. A complex action may be performed using the concatenation of these simple steps.

The most frequent actions that every program must perform are:

- Allocation of values to variables: Suppose that it is needed to work with numeric values 100 and 200. Sentences $x = 100$ and $y = 200$ creates two numeric variables. The values are assigned to them.

- Mathematical operations with the values stored in the variables: The value stored in a variable must be able to be changed the use of mathematical, logical or string operators. If we have $x = 100$ and we want to add 1 to the variable, we just have to say $x=x+1$. This code adds 1 to the previous value of variable x and places it as a new value of the variable. After that, $x=101$-

Examples:

X = Y+1 the new value of X is the value of Y plus 1 unit.

X = Y^2 the new value of X is the squared value of Y

X = X^2 the new value of X is the squared value of the old value of X

X = X*Y the new value of X is the old value of X multiplied by the value of Y

X = X -Y the new value of X is the old value of X minus the value of Y

X = X/Y the new value of X is the old value of X divided by the value of Y

Using these procedures, it is possible to recalculate functions automatically. If we change the value of variable Y, for example, we automatically obtain a new value of variable X.

Logic Conditions: A logic condition consists on a clause that can be responded with the values True or False.

The question: Is X equal to one? (X = 1?) can only be answered with "**True**" or "**False** ".

Conditional Expressions: (Called also IF/THEN/ELSE conditions) Every pseudo-code must have structures that use the conditions in such a way that they express:

If a determined condition happens, **then** *do something.*
If a then certain condition does not happen, **then** *do not do an action.*

Example:

If the value of X is greater than the value of Y then the program finishes
If it is not the database end of file, then go on looking for data
If there is an error, warn the operator about it

If X = 1 then
Y = Y+1
End if

Loops:

Every pseudo-code must have an instruction in order to perform repetitive tasks:
- while a condition is fulfilled
- until a condition is fulfilled
- always
- a certain number of times

Example:

DO (THE FOLLOWING THING) **WHILE** IT FULFILLS A CONDITION

    Order 1
    Order 2

    Order 3

RETURN TO BEGIN

Generically this means that orders 1, 2 and 3 were executed in sequence whereas the specified condition is fulfilled.

Examples:

X = 0
Y = 0
DO WHILE X **IS SMALLER THAN** 1000
Y = Y*X
X = X+1
RETURN

This example accumulates in the variable Y **1000!** (The factorial of 1000: It calculates one thousand times the previous value multiplied by each new digit).
1000! = 1*2*3*4*5......*1000

APPENDIX C

Digitalization of Data

The computers use the binary system for the representation of information, which admits only values of 0 and 1.
In order to turn information to this system, there is a technique that consists of transforming any information into a string of zeros and ones.

The information can exist in different formats:
- Numbers
- Letters
- Computer characters that are neither a letter nor number as the sign "?"
- Photographs
- Drawings in a piece of paper
- X-rays
- Musical tunes
- Radar signals
- Radio signals
- TV signals
- Computed Topography

Case 1: A number

If the information is numerical, it is enough with converting the number to base 2 (binary).

Let's remember that the common numbers are expressed in $base_{10}$, nomenclature that means that:

1234 in $base_{10}$ means that it is made up from the sum of:

$4 \times 10^0 = 4$
$+3 \times 10^1 = 30$
$+2 \times 10^2 = 200$
$+1 \times 10^3 = 1000$

_____

1000+200+30+4=1234

1001 in $base_2$ means that it is made up from the sum of:

$+1 \times 2^0 = 1$
$+0 \times 2^1 = 0$
$+0 \times 2^2 = 0$
$+1 \times 2^3 = 8$

_____

1+0+0+8=9

In other words, 1001 in $base_2$ is equal to 9 in $base_{10}$.

Every number expressed in $base_2$ has its equivalent in $base_{10}$ and vice-versa.

The complete algorithm to turn a binary number into a decimal one can be found in Appendix D.

Case 2-3: A letter or a character that is neither number nor a letter

Some conventions have been made that transform the letters into numbers and vice-versa. One of the best known codes is the ASCII code, that consists of 255 characters corresponding to all the numbers, the letters and the common characters of computer.

Any letter can be transformed into a number using this code, and the resultant numbers can be digitalized using the procedure shown in the previous step.

Cases 4-6: A Photograph , drawing in a piece of paper or X-rays

Scanners are devices that digitalize photos, drawings or X-rays. They divide the photo in thousands of tiny points called pixels. A photography consists in the sum of pixels that it contains.

A number is assigned to each pixel, corresponding to a predefined color scale. We have then a string of numbers, that operate with the procedure shown   in case 1.

The usual color scales have 16 colors, 256 colors or 16 million colors. The size of the resulting string is proportional to the number of colors used. This string is recorded in a computer file and works as shown in case 1.

Case 7-12: Musical tune, Radar, Sonar and Radio signals

Digital sound recorders divide the sonorous melody in very small waves not hearable for the human being and a standard coding number is assigned to them.

The MIDI code is the most popular one for digital music at the moment. This way the sound is converted in a string of numbers, which is managed with the procedure shown in step 1.

Digital reproducers use this string as input, and decode the string in order to reproduce the equivalent sound of each stored number.
In the case of a radar or sonar signal, the bounce of the emitted wave is caught by ad-hoc devices. The treatment is similar as a sonorous wave.

APPENDIX D

Programming activation functions

The objectives of an activation function will vary depending on the objectives and degree of transformation expected by the network designer. The most simple ones only try to standardize the data or convert it into binary strings. As it is said in the body of the book, the election of the activation function is a craftsman choice of the network designer. No one is more recommended than the others for all purposes. Each case must be seen independently. In general, during the first training process, several functions may be proved in order to check which one has a better performance.

The table A4.1 shows some usual functions of activation

TABLE A4.1 Frequent activation functions

Activation Functions	
Logistic Function	$Y = 1/(1+e^{(-x)})$
Decimal to Boolean	$Y = dec2bool(x)$
Decimal to Bipolar	$Y = dec2bip(x)$
Cosine	$Y = cos(x)$
Hyperbolic tangent of X	$Y = tanh(x)$
Hyperbolic tangent of 1,5 X	$Y = tanh(1.5*x)$
Sine	$Y = sin(x)$
Symmetrical Sigmoid	$Y = 2/(1+exp(-x))^{-1}$
Gaussian	$Y = exp(-x^2)$
Complement of Gaussian	$Y = 1 - exp(-x^2)$

Logistic Function:

One of the standard functions used is the sigmoid or logistic function as a default activation function. The function may be used in its original design $Y = 1/(1+e^{(-x)})$, or in any of their variants like $Y = 1/(1+e^{(-x1 * x2)}) + x3$

Programmed in ASP / Visual BASIC:

```
function sigmoid ()
e = 2.718281828459050
sigmoid = 1/(1+e^(sigmo2 * - sigmo1)) +sigmo3
End function
```

Decimal to Boolean function :

This means than the function returns **True** or **False**: A simple function turns input data to format(True/False), symbolized as **0=True–1=False**.

Example: if it is important to know if the values are positive or negative exclusively and we are not interested in their value, it is advisable to turn all positive data to 1 and all the negative values to 0. In this way, a better processing is obtained.

The pseudo-code algorithm for this function is:

```
FUNCTION DECIMAL TO Boolean
Enter a decimal number
If the number is smaller or equal to 0 then return 0
Else return 1
```

We see that the algorithm consists on a condition that returns 1 or 0 depending on the value of the given input number.

The programming of this algorithm ASP/ Visual BASIC is:

Function Dec2bool(deci As Variant) As Double

```
If deci = 0 Then
Dec2bool= 0
Else
Dec2bool = 1
End If
End Function
```

This is a very useful function. However, the zero/one format has this disadvantage: When we multiply any number by zero the result gives zero, reason why the changes in the weights of the network become very abrupt.

In order to avoid this effect, it is common to use a variant of the binary system, with also two possible values. The values are 1 and -1 instead of 0. This system is called " **bipolar** " and has the advantage that there are no null values when we multiply. The following function is a variant of the previous one using bipolar values.

The pseudo-code algorithm for this function is:

```
FUNCTION Dec2bip
Enter a decimal number
If The number is smaller or equal than 0.5 then return -1
Else return 1
End program
```

In ASP / Visual Basic the code is:

```
Function Dec2bip (deci As Variant) As Double
If deci<= 0.5 Then
Dec2bip = - 1
Else
Dec2bip = 1
End If
End Function
```

Another useful function is the Binary to decimal one.

Example: This function returns the decimal number equivalent to a given binary value. It is used in the cases that we must convert the binary results of the net to its decimal equivalency.

In ASP / Visual Basic the code is:

```
Function Binary- to - decimal (b2d As Variant) As Double
b2d = Trim(b2d)
bin2d = 0
lencadena = Len(b2d)
For i = 0 lencadena To - 1
cerouno = Val(Mid(b2d, lencadena - i, 1))
bin2d = bin2d + cerouno * (2 ^ i)
Next
binary - to - decimal = bin2d
End Function
```

APPENDIX E

Neural network's architectures

One of the most important points to consider when we need to program a neural network is the design of a proper network architecture. This is one of the aspects in where the artisan work of the network designer is noted. The chosen network architecture gives a mark, a "signature" that talks about the author. Actually, we can find as many architectures as designers are. Each person will try to add some element to his creation that could confer the network a special characteristic.

Nevertheless, some standard network models exist, which can be used like testing functions. If the prototype of our network does not have a better performance than these networks, then the effort must be continued. If, on the contrary, the new network improves the previous yield, it has reached a fruitful solution for the work.

It is possible to be said that the Back propagation network with a hidden-layer or **BPN (3-layer Back Propagation Network)** is perhaps the most classic structure as a reference network. It consists of three main layers:

In a BPN we find 3 basic elements:

- **The input layer:** It contains the original pattern to be recognized. A weight layer and an activation function are assigned to it.

- **The Hidden layer**: When we multiply the input layer by its weights and we apply the activation function, we get as result the hidden layer values. The hidden layer has also an attached weight layer and it may also have an activation function.
- **The Output layer**: Multiplying the hidden layer by its weights and applying the activation function, we get the output layer values.

The table A5.1 shows the basic scheme of a BPN with a hidden layer

TABLE A5.1 **Basic Scheme of a 3-layer BPN**

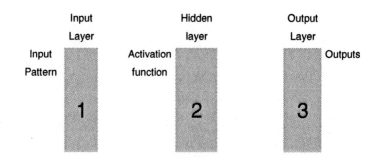

The Table A5.2 shows the data flow scheme of a BPN with a hidden layer

Table A5.2
3-Layer Back Propagation Network

Network Operator or data capture device →	**Input Pattern**	Convert input pattern in a binary string and place it as input layer	Input layer →	Input Layers
		↓Input layer Calculate Hidden Layer values multiplying input layer by its weights and applying the activation function	Input Layer Weights ←	Input-Layer Weights
		↓Hidden Layer Calculate Output Layer values multiplying hidden layer by its weights and applying the activation function	Output Layer Weights ←	Output-Layer Weights
Network Operator ←	**Output value**	↓Output layer value Communicate output layer value to the		

Other Network Architectures:

4-layer Back Propagation Network

It has a similar configuration to the 3-layer BPN, but it has one added extra hidden layer. Therefore, it has one input layer, two hidden layers, and one output layer.

This is also a standard testing network in order to compare its performance with our own prototype. Tables A5.3 and A5.4 shows the basic scheme and the data -flow of a 4-layer Back-propagation Network

TABLE A5.3
Basic Scheme of a 4-layer BPN

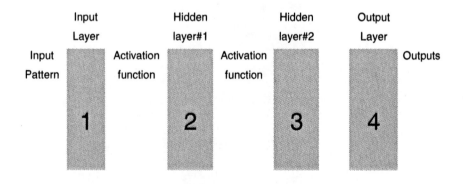

Table A5.4
4-Layer Back Propagation Network

Network Operator or data capture device	Input Pattern →	Convert input pattern in a binary string and place it as input layer		
			Input layer →	_____ Input Layers
		↓Input layer Calculate Hidden Layer #1 values multiplying input layer by its weights and applying the activation function	Input Layer Weights ←	_____ Input-Layer Weights ___ .
		↓Hidden Layer #1 Calculate Hidden Layer #2 values multiplying hidden layer #1 by its weights and applying the activation function	Hidden Layer Weights ←	_____ Hidden-Layer Weights ___ .

↓Hidden Layer

#2

Calculate

Output Layer

values

multiplying   Output Layer
hidden layer by   Weights   Output-Layer
                                       Weights
its weights and   ←

applying the

activation

function

↓Output layer

value

Output   Communicate

value   output layer

Network   value to the
     ←
Operator network

              operator

Jump Connection Networks

It is similar to a BPN but the difference is that each layer is nourished with the previous layers.

In a 3 layer JCN we have:

- **Input layer:** It is nourished of the input patterns.
- **Hidden layer:** It is nourished of the input layer.
- **Output layer:** It is nourished of the hidden layer and the input layer.

In this diagram each circle represents a layer of the network and the emanated arrows the connections. We see that each new layer receives connections of all the previous layers, reason why the training and the execution of the network is slower than a BPN. The more layers it has, the more slower it is to train.

Networks with parallel hidden layers:

In this type of networks, there are one or morel hidden layers in parallel. Each one may contain a different activation function.

As an example, we can think in a network with two hidden layers, each one with a different activation function, both contributing to the network output. Table A5.6
illustrates this architecture.

TABLE A5.6
Basic Scheme of a parallel hidden layers network

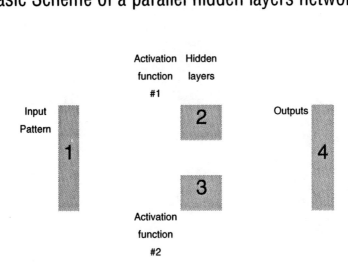

Shape #1 represents the input layer, that receives the input data. Shapes #2 and #3 are the hidden layers in parallel. Each one has its own weights and activation function. The sum of all hidden layers is the input for the output layer.

Self Organization Networks (KOHONEN Network and similar ones)

The characteristic of this networks is that it has only two layers, the input layer and the output layer. Each element of the input layer is associated with an element of the output layer. The Kohonen network is specially useful when we want to group data in categories or classes. Each category, then corresponds to an element of the output layer. Table A5.7 shows a operational diagram of this network.

TABLE A5.7
Basic Scheme of an Self Organization Pattern Network

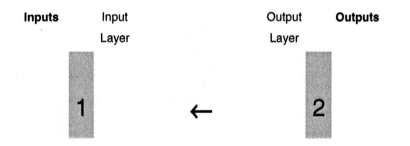

The classic examples where this architecture is useful are the problems where we need to find a match or nexus between the patterns. For example dices symptoms of a disease, are required to know the name the pathology.

Self Associative Memory Networks (SAM)

This type of networks consists of two layers, the input layer and the output layer, but in a way, they are both the same.
This network is similar to the previous one, but has a notable advantage: The input layer is a defective entrance of a pattern and the network tries to return the complete or non defective pattern.

For example: If we look for "John Doe "but by error we enter "John Due", one SAM will give back "John Doe". A SAM network associated to a telephone directory makes possible to write an incorrect name and retrieve back the correct addresses of all the people whose name is similar.

A SAM answers the following question: *"Which are the names in the database that are similar to the one I am entering?"*. If we just talk about text, there are also generic algorithms that perform a similar task. The network, however, can do the same with any pattern, so the recognition is not limited to text. In other words: We can input a digital X-ray pattern with a fracture in a bone and ask the network to find all similar cases stored in the database. Table A5.8 shows the basic scheme of a SAM.

Example: We have used before the shape of the number "1" to work with. In other words: we want to recognize the shape#1

Shape 1

1

We have seen before that when we digitalize the pattern, the computer recognizes a pixels grid such as Shape#2:

Shape 2
0 0 1 0 0
0 1 1 0 0
0 0 1 0 0
0 0 1 0 0
0 1 1 1 0

But now: What happens if the input pattern is Shape#3? We can recognize that it is a defective copy of the Shape#2. The idea is that the computer could be able to do the same.

Shape 3
0 0 1 0 0
0 1 0 0 0
0 0 1 0 0
0 0 1 0 0
0 1 1 0 0

Given a defective input such as Shape#3, a SAM should be able to match it to the correct shape (In this case, shape#2), so, it is expected that the net could identify Shape#3 as the number "1".

This is extremely useful to recognize, for example, text from a dusty Xerox copy, or a scratched piece of paper. When we talked about OCR, (Optical character recognition), we said that the traditional algorithmic methods fail when we are in presence of defective piece of paper or a Xerox copy.

TABLE A5.8
Basic Scheme of a Self Associative Memory Network

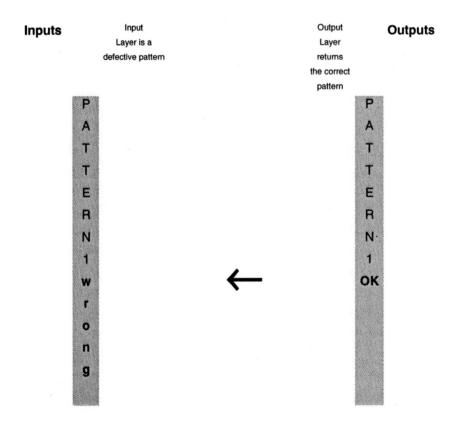

Appendix F

Source Code for a sample Neural Network

In this point we will develop a sample neural network. If you are not a computer programmer, it is recommended for you to skip this part of the book and go to the epilogue.

Startup function:
The startup function is bpn() or trainbpn(), one or the other. Bpn() is just for running the net, and trainbpn() and Bpn2() are for training.

****

*Function **bpn**(bpnpattern)*

'BPN execution complete. No training

st=setup-tables()
if st=true then

forwardpropagate(bpnpattern)
bpn = getoutput()
MsgBox "Output of pattern " & Str(bpnpattern) & " is: " & Str(bpn)

End if

End function

****

Private Function trainbpn(pattern)

```
actualerr = 10000000
acuerror = 1
'modus = "training"
'maxerror= Maximum acceptable error


maxinput = Val(Text7.Text)
If maxinput = 0 Then
maxinput = 2000
End If

maxerror = 1 + (Text6.Text) - 1
If maxerror = 0 Then
maxerror = 0.025
End If

iterations = 0
sec = Now
sqerror = 0

ReDim testbpn(maxinput)
v1 = ""
v2 = ""
v3 = ""
v4 = ""
```

'The first time The net hungs if we put a pattern with a size >text3.text
'that's why I placed 1

```
outputbpn = bpn2(1,maxerror)


Do While iterations <= maxinput

    tt = Left(Right(Format(Now - sec, "ttttt"), 5), 3)

    pir0 = ""
    If iterations > 0 Then
    pir0 = iterations
    End If
    iterations = iterations + 1

    errortotal = 0

    'text3.text i patterns number
    number_patterns = Val(Text3.Text)
    For entre = 1 To number_patterns

    'forward propagation
    outputbpn = bpn2(entre,maxerror)

    'end forward propagation

    'delta outputs
    odt = outdelta(bpntarget(entre), outputbpn)
```

```
'error
actualerr = calcular_error(bpntarget(entre), outputbpn)
errortotal = errortotal + Abs(actualerr)

'delta hidden
x = hidelta(Val(Text4.Text), odt)

'learning speed
omega = (nnet2.Text8.Text)
If (omega = Null Or omega = 0 Or omega = "Text8") Then
MsgBox "Omega=null pasado a 0.5"
omega = 0.5
nnet2.Text8.Text = omega
nnet2.Text8.Refresh
End If

'New weights output
'text4.text is output weights size
x = New_weights_Output(Val(Text4.Text), odt, omega)

'New weights hidden/input
x = New_weights_input(entre, omega)

v1 = Int(outputbpn * 10000) / 10000 & Chr(9) & entre & Chr(13)
v2 = Int(bpntarget(entre) * 10000) / 10000 & Chr(13)
v3 = Int(odt * 10000) / 10000 & Chr(13)
v4 = Int(actualerr * 1000000) / 1000000 & Chr(13) & Int((actualerr
- maxerror) * 10000) / 10000
v5 = Int(errortotal / number_patterns * 1000000) / 1000000


Next
```

```
erroracum = errortotal / number_patterns
testbpn(i) = erroracum

If (erroracum) < maxerror Then
Exit Do
End If

Loop


save_vaues()
trainbpn = 0
End Function
```

****

Function bpn2(bpnpattern, limit)

'BPN for training

```
Setup-tables()
Fill-weights()

Do While Net-Error > limit
forwardpropagate(bpnpattern)              'requires pattern number
```

calc-output-error (Text4.Text)
adjust-weights()
Loop

End function

****

Function setup-tables()
'Erases previous values of the net and loads the new pattern from the tables

'Sets up params

Text2.Text = 9	*'maximum size of each pattern*
Text3.Text = 8	*'total number of patterns stored in the database*
Text4.Text = 3	*'weight size*
Text5.Text = 6	'pattern number to load
Text6.Text = 0.025	'minimum acceptable error
Text7.Text = 1000	'number of iterations before finish training
Text8.Text = 0.5	'learning speed

crit = "delete bpn.* from bpn"
Data1.Database.execute crit
Data1.Refresh
crit = "insert into bpn select bpn-original.* FROM bpn-original "
Data1.Database.execute crit
Data1.Refresh
Data1.Recordset.MoveLast
mess = mess & Chr(13) & "BPN
Records:" &Data1.Recordset.RecordCount

```
crit = "delete bpn-weights.* from bpn-weights"
Data2.Database.execute crit
Data2.Refresh
crit = "insert into bpn-weights select bpn-weights-original.* FROM bpn-
      weights-original "
Data2.Database.execute crit
Data2.Refresh
Data2.Recordset.MoveLast
mess = mess & Chr(13) & "Weights
Records:"&Data2.Recordset.RecordCount

crit = "delete bpn-targets.* from bpn-targets"
Data3.Database.execute crit
Data3.Refresh
crit = "insert into bpn-targets select bpn-targets-original.* FROM bpn-
targets-original "
Data3.Database.execute crit
Data3.Refresh
Data3.Recordset.MoveLast
mess = mess & Chr(13) & "Targets Records:"&Data3.Recordset.RecordCount

setup-tables=true
msgbox mess
end function


*********************************************************


Private Function forwardpropagate(tramano As Variant)
forwardpropagate = propagateinputs(tramano)
End Function
```

****

Private Function propagateinputs(tramanro)

'for a given pattern from the database

'propagate signals from the input layer to the hidden layer

'this means a) calculate the sum of the products of the input layer by their weights . This gives a number
'   b)Apply to this the sigmoid function. This returns a normalized value.

```
outputshidden = "Outputs Hidden " & Chr(13)
sal2 = ""

Redim output_hiddens(Text4.Text)
'text4 is the weight size

sumtotal = 0

For i = 1 To Val(Text4.Text)
    sum = 0
    'text2 is pattern size

    For j = 1 To Val(Text2.Text)
        pir = input_net(j, tramanro)
        pir = pir * input_weights(j, i)
        sum = sum + pir
        sumtotal = sumtotal + pir
    Next
    output_hiddens(i) = sigmoid(sum)
    outputshidden = outputshidden & Str(output_hiddens(i)) & Chr(13)
```

```
Next
If sumtotal = 0 Then
MsgBox outputshidden
End If
propagatelayer = sum
```

End Function
****

Private Function propagateoutput(layernro As Variant)

'for a given pattern from the database

'propagate signals from the hidden layer to the output layer

'this means a) calculate the sum of the products of the hidden layer by their weights . This gives a number
'   *b) Apply to this the sigmoid function. This returns a 'normalized value.*

```
i = layernro
sum = 0
For j = 1 To Val(Text3.Text)
    var001 = input_net(i, j)
    var001 = var001 * input_weights(i, j)
sum = sum + var001
Next
propagateoutput = sigmoid(sum)
```

End Function

****

Function calc-output-error(ok, output)
Calc-output-error = (ok - output)
End Function

****

Function fill-weighs()
'for training only. Fills the tables with Random weights (for the first time).

```
If Val(Text2.Text) = 0 Or Val(Text2.Text) = Null Then
MsgBox "Text2.text Empty"
Exit Sub
End If

If Val(Text4.Text) = 0 Or Val(Text4.Text) = Null Then
MsgBox "Text4.text Empty"
Exit Sub
End If

For i = 1 To Val(Text2.Text)
For j = 1 To Val(Text4.Text)
Data2.Recordset.AddNew
Data2.Recordset.Fields("layer").Value = 1
Data2.Recordset.Fields("row").Value = i
Data2.Recordset.Fields("column").Value = j
Data2.Recordset.Fields("value").Value = Rnd
Data2.Recordset.Update
Next
Next
```

```
For j = 1 To Val(Text4.Text)
Data2.recordset.addnew
Data2.Recordset.Fields("layer").Value = 2
Data2.Recordset.Fields("row").Value = 1
Data2.Recordset.Fields("column").Value = j
Data2.Recordset.Fields("value").Value = Rnd
Data2.Recordset.Update
Next

Data2.Refresh
Data2.Recordset.MoveLast
```

End function

****

Sub setup_target()

```
net-input-number= Data1.Recordset.RecordCount
If net-input-number= 0 Then
MsgBox "Setup Target: bpn table is empty"
Exit Sub
End If
Data1.Recordset.MoveFirst
vrow = 0
vcolumn = 0
vlayer = 0
Do While Not Data1.Recordset.EOF
vrow = IIf(Data1.Recordset.Fields("row").Value > vrow,
Data1.Recordset.Fields("row").Value, vrow)
vcolumn = IIf(Data1.Recordset.Fields("column").Value > vcolumn,
Data1.Recordset.Fields("column").Value, vcolumn)
```

```
'vlayer = IIf(data1.recordset.fields("layer").value > vlayer, data1.record-
set.fields("layer").value, vlayer)
Data1.Recordset.MoveNext
Loop

ReDim bpntarget(vcolumn)


Data1.Recordset.MoveFirst
Do While Not Data1.Recordset.EOF

If Data1.Recordset.Fields("layer").Value = 10 Then
ii = Data1.Recordset.Fields("row").Value
iii = Data1.Recordset.Fields("column").Value
bpntarget(iii) = Data1.Recordset.Fields("valor").Value
End If
Data1.Recordset.MoveNext
Loop
```

End Sub

****

Private Sub setup-input-weights()
```
net-input-number= Data2.Recordset.RecordCount
If net-input-number= 0 Then
MsgBox "Sep input weights: bpn table is empty"
Exit Sub
End If
Data2.Refresh
Data2.Recordset.MoveFirst
vrow = 0
```

```
vcolumn = 0
vlayer = 0
Do While Not Data2.Recordset.EOF
If Data2.Recordset.Fields("layer").Value = 1 Then
vrow    =    IIf(Data2.Recordset.Fields("row").Value    >    vrow,
Data2.Recordset.Fields("row").Value, vrow)
vcolumn = IIf(Data2.Recordset.Fields("column").Value > vcolumn,
Data2.Recordset.Fields("column").Value, vcolumn)
End If

'vlayer = IIf(data1.recordset.fields("layer").value > vlayer, data1.record-
set.fields("layer").value, vlayer)
Data2.Recordset.MoveNext
Loop
'MsgBox "weights" & vrow & vcolumn
'vrow weights text2.text
'vcolumn should be  text4.text
If vrow <> Val(Text2.Text) Then
MsgBox "weight Size detected is = " & Str(vrow) & Chr(13) & "and the
one placed at text2.text is= " & Text2.Text
End If
If vcolumn <> Val(Text4.Text) Then
MsgBox "weights units detected is= " & Str(vcolumn) & Chr(13) & "and
the one placed at text4.text is = " & Text4.Text
End If

Redim input_weights(vrow, vcolumn)
Data2.Recordset.MoveFirst
Do While Not Data2.Recordset.EOF
layer = Data2.Recordset.Fields("layer").Value
ii = Data2.Recordset.Fields("row").Value
iii = Data2.Recordset.Fields("column").Value
```

```
If layer = 1 Then
input_weights(ii, iii) = Data2.Recordset.Fields("valor").Value
End If
Data2.Recordset.MoveNext
Loop

If vcolumn <> Val(Text4.Text) Then
messs = "Weights size detected: " & vcolumn & Chr(13)
messs = messs & "en vez de : " & Text4.Text
x = MsgBox(messs, 48, "Error")
End If
Data2.Recordset.MoveFirst
End Sub
```
****

```
Private Sub setup-inputs()
Data1.Refresh
net-input-number= Data1.Recordset.RecordCount
If net-input-number= 0 Then
MsgBox "Setup Inputs: Bpn table empty"
Exit Sub
End If
Data1.Recordset.MoveFirst
vrow = 0
vcolumn = 0
vlayer = 0
Do While Not Data1.Recordset.EOF

If Data1.Recordset.Fields("layer").Value = 1 Then
vrow = IIf(Data1.Recordset.Fields("row").Value > vrow,
Data1.Recordset.Fields("row").Value, vrow)
```

```
vcolumn = IIf(Data1.Recordset.Fields("column").Value > vcolumn,
Data1.Recordset.Fields("column").Value, vcolumn)
End If

'vlayer = IIf(data1.recordset.fields("layer").value > vlayer, data1.record-
set.fields("layer").value, vlayer)
Data1.Recordset.MoveNext
Loop

'column=pattern number= 8
'row=pattern size=  9
femess = "Patterns" & Chr(13)
Data1.Recordset.MoveFirst
MsgBox femess & Chr(10) & vrow & " " & vcolumn


ReDim input_net(vrow, vcolumn)


Do While Not Data1.Recordset.EOF
layer = Data1.Recordset.Fields("layer").Value
ii = Data1.Recordset.Fields("row").Value
iii = Data1.Recordset.Fields("column").Value
If layer = 1 Then
'MsgBox ii & " " & iii
input_net(ii, iii) = Data1.Recordset.Fields("valor").Value
End If
'If iii = 6 And layer = 1 Then
'femess = femess & input_net(ii, iii) & Chr(13)
'End If
Data1.Recordset.MoveNext
Loop
```

```
'MsgBox femess
Data1.Recordset.MoveFirst
If vrow <> Val(Text2.Text) Then
mess = "Max pattern size detected is  " & vrow & Chr(13)
mess = mess & "en vez de : " & Text2.Text & Chr(13)
mess = mess & "Changing it to " & vrow
Text2.Text = Str(vrow)
x = MsgBox(mess, 48, "Error")
End If

If vcolumn <> Val(Text3.Text) Then
mess = "Pattern number detected is  " & vcolumn & Chr(13)
mess = mess & "en vez de : " & Text3.Text & Chr(13)
mess = mess & "Changing it to: " & vcolumn
Text3.Text = Str(vcolumn)
x = MsgBox(mess, 48, "Error")
End If

End Sub
************************************************************

Private Sub setupweightshidden()
net-input-number= Data2.Recordset.RecordCount
If net-input-number= 0 Then
MsgBox "Setup WeightsHidden: bpn Weights table is empty"
Exit Sub
End If
Data2.Recordset.MoveFirst
vrow = 0
vcolumn = 0
vlayer = 0
Do While Not Data2.Recordset.EOF
```

```
vrow = IIf(Data2.Recordset.Fields("row").Value > vrow,
Data2.Recordset.Fields("row").Value, vrow)
vcolumn = IIf(Data2.Recordset.Fields("column").Value > vcolumn,
Data2.Recordset.Fields("column").Value, vcolumn)
Data2.Recordset.MoveNext
Loop


'ReDim input_net(vrow, vcolumn)

'*****************************************
ReDim weights_hidden(vcolumn)


'ReDim output_hidden(vcolumn)

mess = "Weights Hidden" & Chr(13)
Data2.Recordset.MoveFirst
Do While Not Data2.Recordset.EOF
layer = Data2.Recordset.Fields("layer").Value
If layer = 2 Then
'ii = data2.Recordset.Fields("row").Value
iii = Data2.Recordset.Fields("column").Value
weights_hidden(iii) = Data2.Recordset.Fields("valor").Value


End If

Data2.Recordset.MoveNext
Loop
```

```
If vcolumn <> Val(Text4.Text) Then
mess = "Detected weights from  output layer are " & vcolumn & Chr(13)
mess = mess & "instead of : " & Text4.Text
x = MsgBox(mess, 48, "Error")
End If
```

```
'MsgBox mess
End Sub
```
****

Private Sub store_values()

```
If Data2.Recordset.RecordCount > 0 Then
Data2.Recordset.MoveLast
End If
mess = "There was : " & Str(Data2.Recordset.RecordCount) & "Weights"
crit = "delete bpnweights.* from bpnweights"
Data2.Database.execute crit
Data2.Refresh
```

```
'crit = "insert into bpn select bpnoriginal.* FROM bpnoriginal "
'data1.Database.Execute crit
```

```
totaltosave = 0
'text2.text is pattern number: 9
For i = 1 To Text2.Text
   'text4.text is  weights units=3
   For ihd = 1 To Text4.Text
   Data2.Recordset.AddNew
   'row = 9 column = 3
   Data2.Recordset.Fields("layer").Value = 1
   Data2.Recordset.Fields("row").Value = i
```

```
Data2.Recordset.Fields("column").Value = ihd
Data2.Recordset.Fields("valor").Value = input_weights(i, ihd)

npe = npe & Str(input_weights(i, ihd)) & Chr(13)
totaltosave = totaltosave + input_weights(i, ihd)
Data2.Recordset.Update
Next

Next
If totaltosave = 0 Then
x = MsgBox("No new weights for  hidden layer ", 48, "!!!")
End If
totaltosave = 0

'text4.text es the number of output-weights  = 3
For ihd = 1 To Text4.Text
Data2.Recordset.AddNew
'row = 9 column= 3
Data2.Recordset.Fields("layer").Value = 2
Data2.Recordset.Fields("row").Value = 1
Data2.Recordset.Fields("column").Value = ihd
Data2.Recordset.Fields("valor").Value = weights_hidden(ihd)

totaltosave = totaltosave + weights_hidden(ihd)
Data2.Recordset.Update
Next

If totaltosave = 0 Then
x = MsgBox("No new weights for output layer ", 48, "OJO")
End If
```

```
Data2.Refresh
Data2.Recordset.MoveLast
mess = mess & Chr(13) & "At least there are:" &
Data2.Recordset.RecordCount

MsgBox mess


End Sub
```

****

```
Private Sub Form_Load()
Dim input_net(100, 100)
Dim  weights_hidden(100)
Dim input_weights(100,100)
Dim output_hiddens(100)

End Sub
```

****


```
Private Function new_weights_input(pattern, omega)
npe = ""
totalnpe = 0
'text2.text= pattern size=9
For i = 1 To Text2.Text
    'text4.text is weights size=3
    For ihd = 1 To Text4.Text
    eev = input_net(i, pattern) * omega * vechidelta_rule_(ihd)
    '          9 , 3
    input_weights(i, ihd) = input_weights(i, ihd) + eev
```

```
      npe = npe & Str(input_weights(i, ihd)) & Chr(13)
      totalnpe = totalnpe + input_weights(i, ihd)
      Next
Next
If totalnpe = 0 Then
MsgBox npe
End If
new_weights_input = True
End Function


*********************************************************


Private Function New_weights_Output(outputshidden, delta_rule_out-
puts, omega)


      totalweighthidden = 0
      outwe = "New Weights Output" + Chr(13)
      For ihd = 1 To outputshidden
        weights_hidden(ihd) = 0# + weights_hidden(ihd) + (output_hid-
dens(ihd) * omega * delta_rule_outputs)
      outwe = outwe & Str(weights_hidden(ihd)) & Chr(13)
      totalweighthidden = totalweighthidden + weights_hidden(ihd)
      Next

      If totalweighthidden = 0 Then
      MsgBox outwe
      End If

New_weights_Output = True
End Function
*********************************************************
```

Private Function getoutput()

'text3 is pattern number

'nrooutputnet = Val(Text3.Text)

'redim outputs(nrooutputnet)

' propagate signals to outputs

'we must   a) calculate the sum of the products of the layer multiplied by
                the weights of the output. This gives a number
'   b) apply the sigmoid function to it. This gives a normalized
                number

```
sum = 0
'text4.text is  weights size
For i = 1 To Val(Text4.Text)

      po = weights_hidden(i)
      so = output_hiddens(i)
      sum = sum + po * so
'Next
Next

getoutput = sigmoid(sum)
```

End Function
****
Private Function outdelta_rule(ok, output)

```
outdelta_rule = (ok - output) * output * (1 - output)
End Function
*********************************************************


Private Function sigmoid(sig As Variant)
sigmoid = 1 / (1 + Exp(-sig))
End Function
*********************************************************
```

GLOSSARY

3L-BPN: Three Layer Back-propagation Network. See "Back-propagation Network"

4L-BPN: Four-Layer Back-propagation Network . See "Back-propagation Network"

Activation Function: A computer function that modifies the input layer in order to calculate the hidden layers. It depends on the programmers taste. The election of the activation function is a mark, a craftsman work of the human programmer.

AI: Artificial Intelligence

ANN: Artificial Neural Network. See "Artificial Neural Network"

Artificial Neural Network: A computer software based in the architecture of the biological neural network of the brain. It is specially useful in pattern recognition.

Back-propagation Network: A class of neural network. It has in general one input layer, one output layer and one or more hidden layers. To train it the weights are propagated forward and back creating a recursive feedback training.

BPN: One Hidden Layer Back-propagation Network. See Back-propagation Network

Hidden layer: Intermediate layers of some architectures of neural networks. It can be only one or there can be several ones. It is generally the input layer modified by the activation function and multiplied by the input layer weights.

Input layer: First layer of the neural network. It is generally the input pattern modified in some way to fit the network standards.

JCN: Jump Connection Network. A kind of neural network with several layers. Each of them is connected with all the others.

Layer: Group of artificial neurons. Biological researchers have developed that in the brain the neurons work in groups. The simulation of these groups in the computer is called "neuron layer"

Net: Artificial Neural Network. See "Artificial Neural Network"

Neural Layer: See Layer

Neural Network: Artificial Neural Network. See "Artificial Neural Network"

Nnet: or N-net: Artificial Neural Network. See "Artificial Neural Network"

OCR: Optical Character Recognition.

Optical Character Recognition: A technology that lets a scanner to understand written text and translate it into a computer text file.

Output layer: Last layer of the neural networks. Its value strongly depends on the network specific architecture.

Parallel hidden layers network: A kind of neural network. It is similar to the BPN, but it has hidden layers in parallel. A BPN may have more than one hidden layers, but they are in serial.

PHN: Parallel hidden layers network.

SAM: Self Associative Memory Network.

Self Associative Memory Network: A kind of neural network. It was made to receive defective patters (as text extracted from a Xerox copy in bad condition) and return the correct pattern. It could be seen as a special case of the SOPN, where both patterns are the same.

Self Organization Pattern Network: A kind of neural network. It was made to receive a pattern and match it with another pattern.

SOPN: Self Organization Pattern Network.

Three-Layer Back-propagation Network: See BPN

Weights: In this context, the weight of a layer is a serial of attached values that simulate the strength of the synaptic connections. When a value is multiplied by its weight, it propagates an answer, that is affected by the strength of the weights.

BIBLIOGRAPHY

Author	Description
Ackley D.H.	(1985) A Connectionist algorithm for genetic search page 120-140
Anderson , James & Rosenfeld Edward	(1987) Neuro-computing Cambridge MA MIT Press
Anderson , James & Rosenfeld Edward	(1990) Neuro-computing 2 Cambridge MA MIT Press
Asimov Isaac	(1989) Thoughs about Thought : Essay (In Asimov on Science , A 30 year retrospective 1959, 1989)
Asimov Isaac	(1989) Essay : More Thoughts about Thought. (In Asimov on Science , A 30 year retrospective 1959, 1989)
Asimov Isaac	(1989) Essay about the nature of neural connections "The egg and the shell" (In Asimov on Science , A 30 year retrospective 1959, 1989)
Axelrod R	(1987) The evolution of strategies in the iterated prisoner's dilemma. In Genetic algorithms and simulated annealing page 30-40 London: Pitman
Brock, William A & Hsieh, David A	(1990) A Test for Nonlinear Dynamics Brock, Cambridge MA MIT Press
Burton Robert M	(1992) Event -Dependent Control of noise Enhances Learning in Neural Networks En Neural Networks Vol 5 page 626-637

Author	Description
Caudill M	(1989) Neural Networks Prmer San Francisco CA Miller Freeman Publications
Caudill, M & Butler C	(1990) Naturally Intelligent Systems Cambridge MA MIT Press
Chakraborty , Kanad	(1992) Forecasting the Behavior of Multivariate Time Series Using Neural Networks En Neural Networks Vol 5 page 960-970
Chen J.R.	(1990) Step-size Variation Methods for Accelerating the Back-propagation Algorithm IEEE Proc IJCNN Washington Vol 1 page 601-604
Dawkins Richard	(1993) The selfish gene (The biological base of our behavior) Oxford University Press Reediting
Dayhoff Judith	(1990) Neural Network Architectures :An Introduction New York Van Nostrand Reinhold 1990
Dewdney K A.	(1985) Exploring the field of genetic algorithms in a primordial computer sea full of fibs Scientific American 253(5) 21-32
Duda R. & Hart P	(1993) Pattern Classification and Scene Analysis John Wiley editor
Eberhart Russell C & Dobbins Roy	(1990) Neural Network PC Tools editors London Academic Press
Freeman James	(1993) Neural Networks
Gane y Sarsons	(1982) Structured Systems Analysis
Gately Eduard	(1996) Neural Networks for financial Forecasting Gately Eduard
Goldberg D.E	(1982) SGA A simple Genetic Algorithm Ann Harbor : University of Michigan Department of Civil Engineering

Author	Description
Haykin S	(1991) Adaptable filter Theory NJ Parentice Hall
Jastrow Robert	(1993) The enchanted loom The human brain and the computer Edit: Somon and Schuster Reediting
Jonnson M	(1988) The random walk and Beyond John Wiley editor New York
Kohonen T	(1989) Self Organization and Associative Memory Springer Verlag 3a edition del original 1987
Marina Jose Antonio	(1993) Theory of Creative Intelligence EDT: Anagrama
Miller W. T. y others	(1990) Neural Networks for Robotics and Control Cambridge MA MIT Press
Minsky Marvin & Papert Seymour	(1988) Perceptrons Cambridge MA MIT Press Edition Expanded
Monod Jacques	(1972) Random and Need
Moravec Hans	(1988) The mechanic man. The future of human and robotic intelligence.
Simpson P	(1990) Artificial Neural Systems New York: Pergamon Press
Trillas Eric	(1998) Artificial Intelligence: Men and machines
Weiss Sholom M	(1991) Computer Systems that learn San Mateo CA Morgan Kaufmann

INDEX

0-595-21996-9

Printed in the United States
18084LVS00003B/181